THE 40-DAY SURRENDER FAST

Journal

Scriptures and Reflections from
The 40-Day Surrender Fast

Celeste Owens, Ph.D.
with Stephanie B. Davis

Good Success Publishing

The 40-Day Surrender Fast

Requests for information should be addressed to:
Good Success Publishing, P.O. Box 134, Oxon Hill, MD 20750-0134

ISBN: 978-0-9837895-3-6 (softcover)

Library of Congress Control Number: 2011933636

This book is printed on acid-free paper.

Cover design: Pixel Ink Studios
Interior design: Compass Rose Horizons

Printed in the United States of America

I Commit to Surrender for Life

Your Name

Date Surrendered

CONTENTS

Pre-Fast Preparation

PRE-FAST PREPARATION

Let God Do a New Thing!

Point to ponder: I won't leave this year the same way I came in. The former things have passed; God wants to do a new thing in me.

Scriptures to reference: Isaiah 43:18-19.

Personal Reflections

1. What "new thing" does God want to do in and for me?

2. I sense God asking me to give up some tasks or jobs that are important to me? What are they? Will I comply?

3. What role, if any, will fear play in hindering me from allowing God to do the new thing in my life?

Prayer request(s):

How my prayer(s) was answered?

PRE-FAST PREPARATION

What Is a Surrender Fast?

Point to ponder: I will no longer be stuck, frustrated, or bound. I am going to let God do something new in me and the blessings that will stem from my obedience will be well worth the sacrifice.

Scriptures to reference: Matthew 4:1-11; Deuteronomy 28.

Personal Reflections

1. Dr. Celeste was introduced to fasting as a child and has continued the practice into adulthood. However, some new or even seasoned converts for that matter don't regard fasting as beneficial. What are my thoughts about fasting? When I have fasted in the past did it produce the results I expected? What do I expect from a Surrender Fast?

2. What area(s) of my life do I need to surrender to God? What will be most challenging about surrendering?

3. How might this surrender change my relationship with God, myself, and others?

Prayer request(s):

How my prayer(s) was answered?

PRE-FAST PREPARATION

Bold and Courageous

Point to ponder: I am healed from the pains and wounds of the past; I am new in Christ, and equipped to succeed in all that I put my hands to.

Scriptures to reference: Isaiah 61:7; Isaiah 54:3-6.

Personal Reflections

1. Have I decided what I will surrender for the next 40 days? (If yes, write answer below). If not, that is okay; I have time. I will simply continue to seek God's direction and He will give me the answer.

2. Like Dr. Celeste, who was encouraged by the words God spoke to Joshua, how has God prepared my heart for the Surrender Fast?

3. The enemy wants me to be ashamed of my weaknesses and to hide them from others, but that philosophy only delays my healing. Therefore, I am going to identify a weakness and make arrangements to talk with at least one other person about it. I'll ask him/her to hold me accountable (through the duration of the fast) as I allow God to change me in this area.

   [Practical tip: If you can't readily identify a person that can be part of this process with you, pray. God will reveal the right person to you. When He does go to that person, explain what you are doing, and ask them to be part of this journey with you. Write the name of that person here.]

Prayer request(s):

How my prayer(s) was answered?

PRE-FAST PREPARATION

Why 40 Days?

Point to ponder: In and of myself I am hopeless to change, but with God all things are possible. His healing virtue is tearing down the walls that have kept me confined and His grace is propelling me further than I ever thought I could go.

Scriptures to reference: Mark 9:14-29; Genesis 7:4; Joshua 5:6; 1 Samuel 17:16; 2 Samuel 5:4; 1 Kings 2:11; Matthew 4:2; Luke 4:2; Mark 1:14.

Personal Reflections

1. What behaviors or circumstances keep me bound and also act as a barrier to the life God has for me?

2. Do I believe that God can deliver me from any and every stronghold? There's a habit I would like to eliminate. What have I tried in the past to rid myself of this problem? Has the problem gotten better over time or remained the same? How will I know when God has healed me?

3. Am I willing to commit to this period of fasting for 40 days? What people or circumstances might negatively impact my ability to succeed at this fast?

Prayer request(s):

How my prayer(s) was answered?

PRE-FAST PREPARATION

It's Complicated

Point to ponder: I don't need anyone to approve of or accept me because God loves me just the way I am. If I meditate on His word day and night, do all that it says, I will make my way prosperous and I will have good success.

Scriptures to reference: Joshua 1:8; 2 Corinthians 10:5; I John 4:19.

Personal Reflections

1. What lies, if any, from childhood have I accepted as truth? In what ways do they continue to influence my thoughts and behavior?

2. Do these lies also affect my current relationships? If yes, with whom and in what way?

3. How would I like for God to change me over the next 40 days?

Prayer request(s):

How my prayer(s) was answered?

DAY 1

Expect the Unexpected

"For My thoughts *are* not your thoughts,
nor *are* your ways my ways," says the LORD.
"For *as* the heavens are higher than the earth,
So are My ways higher than your ways,
And My thoughts than your thoughts.
(Isaiah 55:8-9)

Point to ponder: Growth won't occur by osmosis; a dream comes with much business and painful effort. If I want to experience a new thing in God, I must do my part.

Scriptures to reference: Ecclesiastes 4:3; Psalm 25:9, 69:32, 147:6; James 4:10; I Peter 5:6; Isaiah 55:8-9.

Personal Reflections

1. From the start, God is instructing me to be humble. What does humility mean to me? How is it related to the act of surrender?

2. Sometimes I'm afraid to display humility because I associate meekness with weakness. Is there a difference between humility and being a pushover? Explain.

3. On a scale from one to ten, what is my commitment level to reading God's word daily, reading this devotional, and praying?

Prayer request(s):

How my prayer(s) was answered?

DAY 2

Time, Effort, Reward

Sow for yourselves righteousness;
Reap in mercy;
Break up your fallow ground,
For *it is* time to seek the LORD,
Till He comes and rains righteousness on you.
(Hosea 10:12)

Point to ponder: The new thing I seek is here, but my possession of it requires time and effort. This little investment of my time will reap an abundant reward!

Scriptures to reference: Hosea 10:12; Galatians 6:7; II Corinthians 9:6.

Personal Reflections

1. What sacrifices will I make in order to draw closer to God?

2. Typically, what is my commitment level when it comes to starting new regiments? Am I readily committed to a plan from the beginning and follow it through to the end? Or am I commitment phobic? If the latter, what do I fear?

3. Scenario #1: I identified fears; therefore, I'll discuss them with my accountability partner. I'll also pray and ask God to strengthen me so that I'm able to push through the fear and succeed to the finish. This is how my accountability partner responded to our conversation:

   Scenario #2: I'm naturally a committed person and I thank God for this gift. Now I am asking Him to use me to help develop this character trait in others. This is how He will use me in this area:

Prayer request(s):

How my prayer(s) was answered?

DAY 3

Rebuild and Renew

And they shall rebuild the old ruins,
they shall raise up the former desolations,
And they shall repair the ruined cities,
The desolations of many generations.
(Isaiah 61:4)

Point to ponder: My radical act of faith is doing the impossible. My surrender delights God.

Scriptures to reference: Ephesians 3:20; Psalm 37:4; Isaiah 61

Personal Reflections

1. Dr. Celeste mentioned some of the benefits of surrendering: more intimate relationship with God, improved emotional health, and breakthroughs in many other areas of my life. What are other benefits?

2. What impossible thing has God done for me in the past? How did it increase my faith?

3. What "abundant thing" am I expecting God to do for me and my family as a result of this fast? I am asking Him to break these negative generational patterns. Do I believe that He can and will do it?

Prayer request(s):

How my prayer(s) was answered?

DAY 4

The Other Side

On the same day, when evening had come, He said to them,
"Let us cross over to the other side."
(Mark 4:35)

Point to ponder: Whatever He has asked me to release to Him is His will and I will succeed.

Scriptures to reference: I Corinthians 2:9; Mark 4:35-41.

Personal Reflections

1. What storms have begun in my life as a result of my surrender?

2. What can the disciples teach me about enduring the storm?

3. Like Dr. Celeste, is God requiring me to step out of my comfort zone to do some activities that I've been fearful of doing? How long have I avoided this activity? Will I finally heed His voice?

Prayer request(s):

How my prayer(s) was answered?

DAY 5

It Will Come to Pass

Every word of God *is* pure;
He *is* a shield to those who put their trust in Him.
(Proverbs 30:5)

Point to ponder: God's word will not return to Him void.

Scriptures to reference: I John 3:2a; Matthew 25:23; Zechariah 4:10; Joshua 21:45, 23:14; Proverbs 30:5

Personal Reflections

1. What promises has God spoken to me that have yet to come to pass? Do I believe that He will do just as He has said?

2. What preparations am I making for the manifestation of each promise?

3. Sometimes as I wait I become anxious for the manifestation of God's plan. Am I content with today or anxious for tomorrow? If the latter, what will I do to maintain balance as I wait?

Prayer request(s):

How my prayer(s) was answered?

DAY 6

Personal Reflection

DAY 7

Personal Reflection

DAY 8

Establish Your Faith

And whatever you ask in My name, that I will do,
that the Father may be glorified in the Son.
If you ask anything in My name, I will do *it*.
(John 14:13-14)

Point to ponder: Faith is more than mere words; it is an attitude of confidence that knows without a shadow of a doubt that God will do just as He has promised.

Scriptures to reference: James 2:20, 3:10, Hebrews 11:6; Proverbs 18:21; John 14:13-14

Personal Reflections

1. Establishing or activating my faith is only possible when I believe that God will do just what He has said. How convinced am I that God will work things out for my good? In which areas of my life do I need to trust God more?

2. The scripture tells me that faith without works is dead (see James 2:26). What does that mean to me? In which areas of my life do I need to establish my faith?

3. There is power in sharing with another trusted individual what I believe God will do for me. I'll tell my accountability partner what I'm expecting God to do.

Prayer request(s):

How my prayer(s) was answered?

DAY 9

Pray for Your Enemies

Do not rejoice when your enemy falls,
And do not let your heart be glad when he stumbles;
Lest the LORD see *it,* and it displease Him,
And He turn away His wrath from him.
(Proverbs 24:17-18)

Point to ponder: It's easy to love those who love me, but the proof of my conversion is reflected in my ability to love those who use me, who take advantage of my kindness, and wish harm upon me.

Scriptures to reference: Matthew 5:44; Philippians 4:13; Proverbs 24:17-18

Personal Reflections

1. I'll pray and ask God to reveal to me the condition of my heart. A prayer that Dr. Celeste said she often whispers is, "God show me, me." Is He revealing to me a person or persons that I have not forgiven? If yes, what will I do to make this right?

2. Forgiveness for those who have hurt me goes against my nature. Why then does God require that I forgive? What are the benefits of forgiving? What are the consequences of unforgiveness? What scriptures validate my answers?

3. What does Christ's sacrifice mean to me and how does it demonstrate how I'm to love?

Prayer request(s):

How my prayer(s) was answered?

DAY 10

Renewal is Necessary

And He said to them,
"Come aside by yourselves to a deserted place and rest a while."
For there were many coming and going,
and they did not even have time to eat.
(Mark 6:31)

Point to ponder: God wants me to live in the peace that surpasses all understanding, to have unspeakable joy, and to prosper in all things.

Scriptures to reference: Mark 6:30-32

Personal Reflections

1. Based on Dr. Celeste's definition, am I primarily busy or primarily productive? If prone to busyness what would I say drives my behavior and motivates me to keep up a pattern of busyness? If, however, I'm mostly productive, what safeguards have I put in place to maintain this balanced lifestyle?

2. When I'm busy for the sake of being busy, how is pride driving my behavior?

3. Am I getting enough rest? If not, what will I do to make this a regular part of my daily renewal?

4. What activities or circumstances is the Holy Spirit urging me to eliminate? Are there certain relationships I need to sever? Will I obey His leading?

Prayer request(s):

How my prayer(s) was answered?

DAY 11

Peculiar Am I

But ye are a chosen generation, a royal priesthood,
an holy nation, a peculiar people;
that ye should shew forth the praises of him who hath
called you out of darkness
into his marvellous light;
(I Peter 2:9, KJV)

Point to ponder: God is preparing me for my next phase in Him, but I must first accept the "me" that He has called me to be.

Scriptures to reference: I Peter 2:4-10

Personal Reflections

1. Can I relate to Dr. Celeste's sentiment about being different? If so, in what ways am I different, and am I okay with that?

2. What personality or character traits do I find most challenging to accept?

3. In what way might being different positively influence my ability to fulfill the call that God has on my life?

4. I have the power to speak life. Identify at least one person I can encourage that is struggling with being different? What will I say to encourage him/her? What portion of my testimony could I share that would help them embrace their uniqueness?

Prayer request(s):

How my prayer(s) was answered?

DAY 12

God's Friend

I love those who love me,
And those who seek me diligently will find me.
(Proverbs 8:17)

Point to ponder: Gro A meaningful relationship with God includes seeking His advice first.

Scriptures to reference: Isaiah 58:9a; Proverbs 8:17

Personal Reflections

1. What is my first reaction when I have a dilemma? Do I first discuss it with family and friends then go to God or do I go to God first?

2. God speaks to all of us differently, but He can often be heard as a still small voice speaking to our spirits. Have I learned to hear God's voice for myself?

3. How do I know when He is speaking to me? Besides a still small voice, what other ways could He speak to me?

4. Do I consider myself God's friend? What steps will I take to draw even closer to Him?

Prayer request(s):

How my prayer(s) was answered?

DAY 13

Personal Reflection

DAY 14

Personal Reflection

DAY 15

I Declare War!

For we do not wrestle against flesh and blood, but against principalities, against powers, against the rulers of the darkness of this age, against spiritual *hosts* of wickedness in the heavenly *places*.
(Ephesians 6:12, KJV)

Point to ponder: I won't take Satan's tactics lying down; I'll get on my knees and exercise the authority that Christ has given me.

Scriptures to reference: I John 4:4; James 4:7; Ephesians 6:10-12

Personal Reflections

1. Spiritual warfare is real. The enemy is determined to discourage me from completing this fast. In what ways has my faith been challenged? What safeguards have or will I put in place to secure a successful completion of this fast?

2. It always helps to recall past victories. Have there been other times that I felt like I was in a war or spiritual battle? What was the outcome? What did I do to stay strengthened?

3. What I believe is often evident in how I behave. Earlier, Dr. Celeste mentioned how important it is to exhibit self-control, especially when it comes to controlling your emotions. How am I behaving during this fast? Am I grumbling and complaining or am I confident and positive?

4. Do I wholeheartedly believe that God has given me power over the enemy? If yes, do my thoughts and behavior reflect a heart of belief?

Prayer request(s):

How my prayer(s) was answered?

DAY 16

Superhuman

But those who wait on the LORD
Shall renew *their* strength;
They shall mount up with wings like eagles,
They shall run and not be weary,
They shall walk and not faint.
(Isaiah 40:31)

Point to ponder: Today I declare that I can be super human if I simply wait on God and let His supernatural power work in my life.

Scriptures to reference: Isaiah 40:26-31, 55:11

Personal Reflections

1. How am I at waiting? Do I want everything right now or have I learned to wait on God? In what ways can I improve my attitude during the wait time?

2. What am I waiting for the Lord to do in my life? How long have I been waiting? What is most challenging about the wait? Do I trust God to do what He said He would do?

3. Like Dr. Celeste, have I ever received news about a situation that was contrary to the word that God had given me? What did I do? Did I compromise or did I wait? What was the outcome?

Prayer request(s):

How my prayer(s) was answered?

DAY 17

The God in Me

The ark of the LORD remained in the house of
Obed-Edom the Gittite three months.
And the LORD blessed Obed-Edom and all his household.
(II Samuel 6:11)

Point to ponder: If I'm willing to endure a little discomfort for a season, others will have the awesome opportunity to see God in me and be blessed beyond measure.

Scriptures to reference: II Corinthians 3:17 (NKJV); II Samuel 6:11

Personal Reflections

1. Have I been or am I now in a place where I would rather not be? Explain?

2. If I'm in a challenging situation now, am I representing God well?

3. Are others being blessed because I'm in their presence? Are they able to see the love of God radiating from me? If not, what will I do to be a better representation of God?

Prayer request(s):

How my prayer(s) was answered?

DAY 18

The Keys for Good Relationships

Behold, how good and how pleasant *it is*
for brethren to dwell together in unity!
(Psalm 133:1)

Point to ponder: God designed me to be in healthy relationships and to dwell in unity.

Scriptures to reference: Matthew 18:15a; Psalm 133

Personal Reflections

1. How would I rate the quality of my relationships? Are they healthy and thriving or challenging and conflict-filled? What can I do to improve my relationships?

2. Is one or more of my relationships strained? What caused the strain and how did I play a part in all of this? What will I do to make it right?

3. Ultimately, the quality of my relationships is a reflection of the relationship I have with God. What is my relationship like with God? Am I making time to seek Him?

4. If you don't love yourself, loving someone else is nearly impossible. How do you feel about you? Are there some unresolved issues that you need to address? Where will you start? Speak with your accountability partner about what the spirit is revealing to you about yourself.

Prayer request(s):

How my prayer(s) was answered?

DAY 19

I Still Surrender

And they overcame him by the blood of the Lamb
and by the word of their testimony.
(Revelation 12:11a)

Point to ponder: I will be the victor if I faint not. I'm almost to the finish line; I'll see it through to the end.

Scriptures to reference: Psalm 139:14; Revelations 12:11

Personal Reflections

1. Have I been tempted to give up on this fast? How do I think my continued surrender will benefit me in the long run?

2. We all have had struggles. What childhood challenges influence the way I operate as an adult?

3. Sometimes it's embarrassing to share with another person what I'm struggling with, but the scripture tells me that I've overcome by the words of my testimony. Share with my accountability partner or other close friend one of my current challenges. How difficult will that be? How do I think it will help me?

Prayer request(s):

How my prayer(s) was answered?

DAY 20

Personal Reflection

DAY 21

Personal Reflection

DAY 22

Dust Off Your Dreams

For a dream comes through much activity,
and a fool's voice *is known* by *his* many words.
(Ecclesiastes 5:3)

Point to ponder: Trust that God has it all handled and He will provide the means. All He needs from me is my willingness to comply with His every command.

Scriptures to reference: Habakkuk 2:2-4; Ecclesiastes 5:3

Personal Reflections

1. What are my dreams? (Write them down.) Am I on the road to fulfilling them? If not, what is holding me back?

2. Review my list, choose one dream and write out the specific steps that I'll need to take to make this dream a reality.
   For example: *I want to be a Surgical Tech*
   Step 1 — Research the qualification needed to be a Surgical Tech
   Step 2 — Talk with a Surgical Tech to get their opinion about a field
   Step 3 — Apply to schools.

3. For many different reasons, people fear telling others about their dreams. I won't be fearful. I'll pick one of the dreams I listed in Question 2. Tell either my accountability partner or close friend about that dream.

4. How did it feel to tell someone else? How did they respond?

Prayer request(s):

How my prayer(s) was answered?

DAY 23

Your Breakthrough Is Coming Through

Then it happened, as he drew back his hand,
that his brother came out unexpectedly;
and she said, "How did you break through?
This breach *be* upon you!"
Therefore his name was called Perez.
(Genesis 38:29)

Point to ponder: I am the Victor and not the conquered, the Head and not the tail, Above and not beneath.

Scriptures to reference: Matthew 1:3a; Deuteronomy 28; Genesis 38

Personal Reflections

1. Am I in need of a breakthrough? Do I believe that God can and will deliver me from whatever I'm challenged by right now? What will I do to keep my faith strong?

2. Who has been my "Judah"? What did they do? In what way, if any, does this hurt still affect me today?

3. God doesn't waste pain. Tamar was rewarded handsomely for the hurt that she endured at the hand of Judah. Can I see how the hurts of my life have been or will be for God's greater plan? If not, I'll pray and ask God to open the eyes of my heart so that I can see some of what He has in store for me.

Prayer request(s):

How my prayer(s) was answered?

DAY 24

The Answered Prayer

Then Eli answered and said,
"Go in peace, and the God of Israel grant your petition
which you have asked of Him."
(I Samuel 1:17)

Point to ponder: I'll be content with today, praise God for what He has already done, and wait expectantly, without worry, for what is to come.

Scriptures to reference: I Peter 3:12; I Samuel 1:8-18

Personal Reflections

1. What specific requests have you put before God during the course of this fast? Do you believe that He will answer your prayers?

2. How is your thought life? During times of stress, do you allow the enemy to bombard you with negative thoughts? Do you find solace in complaining? If you answered yes to either of those questions, what might you do differently the next time you are stressed about a particular situation?

Prayer request(s):

How my prayer(s) was answered?

DAY 25

The Dead Will Live

As soon as Jesus heard the word that was spoken,
He said to the ruler of the synagogue,
"Do not be afraid; only believe."
(Mark 5:36)

Point to ponder: It ain't over, until God says it's over. He has the final say.

Scriptures to reference: Romans 4:17; Joel 2:25-26; Proverbs 24:10; Mark 5:21-43

Personal Reflections

1. We are all in need of prayer. Name the specific ways my accountability partner can pray for me this week then ask him/her to pray with me.

2. Can I recall a time when I thought all hope was lost yet God resurrected a dead situation in my life? What was that situation and how did God turn it around for me?

3. The Word says that if I faint in the day of adversity my strength is small (see Proverbs 24:10). How do I handle adversity? Do I give up easily or forge ahead knowing that God has the final say?

4. Do I currently have a dead situation in my life? What is it? Do I believe that God can resurrect it?

Prayer request(s):

How my prayer(s) was answered?

DAY 26

What Is for Me Is for Me

He shall be like a tree
Planted by the rivers of water,
that brings forth its fruit in its season,
whose leaf also shall not wither;
and whatever he does shall prosper.
(Psalm 1:3)

Point to ponder: When we walk according to God's plan we can't miss out.

Scriptures to reference: II Corinthians 10:1-6; Psalm 1:3, 37:4, 23; Isaiah 55:11; Psalm 37:4; Deuteronomy 28:1-2

Personal Reflections

1. The mind is the battleground of the enemy. How often do I allow the enemy to have free reign of my thoughts? What will I do to gain better control over what I'm thinking?

2. How confident am I that what God has for me is for me? Are there times when I compare myself to others and become discouraged? How has God proven to me that His plan for me will come to pass?

3. List some of the promises that God has made me. Thank Him for these promises and ask Him to give me peace as I patiently wait for the manifestation of His promises.

Prayer request(s):

How my prayer(s) was answered?

DAY 27

Personal Reflection

DAY 28

Personal Reflection

DAY 29

The God of the Impossible

But Jesus looked at *them* and said to them,
"With men this is impossible, but with God all things are possible."
(Matthew 19:26)

Point to ponder: In this season, God is calling me to a level of radical faith that far exceeds my previous dealings with Him.

Scriptures to reference: Luke 17:6; John 14:13-14; Matthew 19:23-30

Personal Reflections

1. What is faith? How has God tested my faith recently? What was the situation? Did the test draw me closer to God or cause me to move away. What do I need to do to increase my faith in God?

2. What bold and courageous declarations will I make today? What impossible thing do I believe God will do for me?

3. Sometimes in our zeal we overstate God's will. How will I feel at the end of the fast if things don't turn about the way I envisioned? Will I still trust God to do the impossible?

Prayer request(s):

How my prayer(s) was answered?

DAY 30

Little Time Needed

"For My thoughts *are* not your thoughts,
nor *are* your ways my ways," says the LORD.
(Isaiah 55:8)

Point to ponder: God doesn't need a lot of time.

Scriptures to reference: Jeremiah 17:5-8; Isaiah 55:8

Personal Reflections

1. Yesterday's blog post asked me to write down what I believe God will do for me before this fast's end. Did I do that? If not, what stopped me from making a declaration?

2. The old saying goes, "He may not come when you want, but He is always on time." Do I believe this to be true? Can I recall a time when I thought all hope was gone? Did things eventually work out for me? What lessons did I learn from that particular circumstance?

3. On a scale from one to ten, what is my commitment level to reading God's word daily, reading this devotional, and praying?

Prayer request(s):

How my prayer(s) was answered?

DAY 31

Grace and Glory

For by grace you have been saved through faith,
and that not of yourselves;
it is the gift of God, not of works, lest anyone should boast.
(Ephesians 2:8-9)

Point to ponder: Without God's grace we would still be dead in our sins, wallowing in a sea of defeat and desperation.

Scriptures to reference: James 1:5; Ephesians 2:1-10

Personal Reflections

1. As the song implies, "All the glory belongs to God." What does that mean to me? Take a moment to write down one thing God has done for me in the last week; the last month; and the last year.

2. Am I one to allow God's grace to operate in my life or do I try to do most things in my own strength?

3. Have I or am I now in God's way? Identify how.

4. For which challenging situations do I need to leave more room for God's grace to operate? What will I do so that God has complete control?

Prayer request(s):

How my prayer(s) was answered?

DAY 32

Act Like You Are About to Move

"Pass through the camp and command the people, saying,
'Prepare provisions for yourselves, for within three days
you will cross over this Jordan, to go in to possess
the land which the LORD your God is giving you to possess.'"
(Joshua 1:11)

Point to ponder: Step out in faith; prepare my provisions, and ACT LIKE I'm ABOUT TO MOVE.

Scriptures to reference: Joshua 1:10-18; Habakkuk 2:2-3

Personal Reflections

1. What does the phrase ACT LIKE YOU ARE ABOUT TO MOVE mean to me?

2. It is said that preparation plus opportunity equals success. Think of one dream that God has placed in my heart. In what ways am I preparing for the manifestation of that dream?

3. What signs have God shown me to let me know that He is ready to work on my behalf?

Prayer request(s):

How my prayer(s) was answered?

DAY 33

The Promise

And everyone who has left houses
or brothers or sisters or father or mother or wife or children or lands,
for my name's sake, shall receive a hundredfold, and inherit eternal life.
(Matthew 19:29)

Point to ponder: If I would allow Gods' grace to empower my every action, God will get the glory, and I will receive all that God has promised, even a hundredfold." Amen.

Scriptures to reference: Exodus 20:2-3; Ephesians 3:20; Matthew 19:23-30

Personal Reflections

1. What sacrifices have I made in the past? In what way(s) did God reward me for my sacrifice(s)?

2. Are there people or situations that I put before God? If yes, who are they and what will I do to make this right?

3. How do I feel about there being one last week? Has this process helped me to feel closer to God? Have I noticed changes in others and myself? List those changes here.

Prayer request(s):

How my prayer(s) was answered?

DAY 34

Personal Reflection

DAY 35

Personal Reflection

DAY 36

No More Props

FOR BEHOLD, the Lord, the Lord of hosts,
is taking away from Jerusalem and from Judah the stay
and the staff [every kind of prop],
the whole stay of bread and the whole stay of water,
(Isaiah 3:1, Amplified Bible)

Point to ponder: Depending solely on other people to hear a word from God is childish. It is time that I hear, believe, and speak God's truth as He has spoken it to me.

Scriptures to reference: I Corinthians 13:11; Isaiah 3:1

Personal Reflections

1. What are the props that are in my life?

2. A benefit of releasing my props is the ability to hear God for my-self and to have a closer, more intimate relationship with Him. Is God telling me that it is time to let Him remove the props? Am I willing to let go? Why or why not?

3. What do I anticipate life will be like without the props?

Prayer request(s):

How my prayer(s) was answered?

DAY 37

Reject Rejection

"Whoever listens to you listens to me; whoever rejects you rejects me; but whoever rejects me rejects him who sent me."
(Luke 10:16)

Point to ponder: He will use me to call into existence that which is not, to move mountains in faith, and to draw men to Him.

Scriptures to reference: Luke 10:1-20

Personal Reflections

1. How do I handle rejection? Am I easily wounded by another's rejection or can I shake it off and move on? If the former, how will the scriptures in Luke 10 help me to better deal with rejection?

2. Do I sense God calling me to do something radical like Dr. Celeste's dad? What is it? Will I be obedient to God's command?

3. Isn't being reminded that the demons are subject to Jesus encouraging? Will this truth allow me to release fear so that I will able to follow God's commands no matter the potential for rejection?

4. In which area of my life will I work on releasing fear?

Prayer request(s):

How my prayer(s) was answered?

DAY 38

Childlike Humility

Therefore, whoever takes the lowly position of this child
is the greatest in the kingdom of heaven.
(Matthew 18:4)

Point to ponder: That is what my heavenly father requires of me: a complete surrender and trust of His plan.

Scriptures to reference: Revelation 2:17; Matthew 18:1-5

Personal Reflections

1. How is surrendering my will a demonstration of humility?

2. Why do I think humility is so important to God? In which areas of my life could I exercise more humility?

3. Humility is necessary for me to be in a healthy relationship(s). Romans 12:3 reads, "For I say, through the grace given to me, to everyone who is among you, not to think *of himself* more highly than he ought to think, but to think soberly, as God has dealt to each one a measure of faith." How do you think having humility in your relationships will strengthen them?

Prayer request(s):

How my prayer(s) was answered?

DAY 39

Wait on the Lord

"So I will restore to you the years that the swarming locust has eaten,
the crawling locust,
the consuming locust,
and the chewing locust,
my great army which I sent among you.
And praise you shall eat in plenty and be satisfied,
the name of the LORD your God,
Who has dealt wondrously with you;
and my people shall never be put to shame."
(Joel 2:25-26)

Point to ponder: Wait on the Lord and be of good courage.

Scriptures to reference: I Kings 8:56; Joshua 21:45; Joel 2:18-27

Personal Reflections

1. God will restore all that the locust has eaten. What area(s) of my life are in need of repair and restoration?

2. During the course of this fast, how has God made changes in my circumstances?

3. How do I see God continuing to restore over the course this year? In five years? In ten years?

Prayer request(s):

How my prayer(s) was answered?

DAY 40

God Has Done a New Thing

I am appropriately silenced this morning. I simply hear God saying,
"Oh, give thanks to the LORD!"
(Psalm 105:1a)

Take the time this morning and throughout the weekend to reflect on what God has done during these 40-days. I pray that you have allowed Him to do a new thing in you. Be blessed!

About the Authors

Dr. Celeste Owens. Once, a little girl in the 7th grade read something about someone else's pain. Her purpose was clear, to help those that have been hurt and mangled by life. It was in that moment that Celeste knew she would become a psychologist. Her sensitivity to the distress of others framed her life purpose to assist in improving the quality of life for all those who God allowed to her to intercept paths with.

Dr. Celeste practiced as a psychologist for more than 10 years, but when God instructed her to leave it all behind, she did. Today she is reaping the benefits of her obedience. Although her career focus has changed -- she is now a Motivational Speaker, Health Advocate, and Author -- her passion to help others live his/her best life has not.

In 2012, she and her husband Andel co-founded Dr. Celeste Owens Ministries, LLC who's calling hearts back to God through surrender of mind, body, and spirit. They believe that surrender is a lifestyle and a necessary posture for today's Christian.

An accomplished scholar, Dr. Celeste holds a Bachelor of Arts in Psychology from the State University of New York at Buffalo, a Master of Science in Applied Counseling Psychology from the University of Baltimore and a Doctorate of Philosophy in Counseling Psychology from the University of Pittsburgh. In 2013, Dr. Celeste became a Certified Natural Health Professional.

Dr. Celeste resides in the surrounding Washington Metropolitan Area where her most important works are being wife to her husband of 13 years and mom to their two children.

Stephanie B. Davis. Mrs. Davis is the Executive Administrative Assistant to Dr. Celeste Owens. She is also an active member of her church, The Latter Rain Cathedral, and loving wife and mom to her husband Frank and son Ethan. They reside in the Western New York area.

Mrs. Davis is a Certified Natural Health Professional. In her spare time she loves sharing her expertise on health and wellness. Check out her contributions to the Surrender Blog at www.drcelesteowensblog.com.